The Ultimate Guide for Teenage Fun!

WRITTEN BY SHELLEY WILLE
ILLUSTRATED BY CRAIG HARRIS

Shelley Wille attended both Ricks College and Brigham Young University majoring in Family Life Education. She is an author, lecturer, homemaker, and mother of six children.

Dr. Craig Harris attended school at B.Y.U, the University of North Carolina, and the University of Washington. He currently resides in Saline, Michigan, where he teaches at the University of Michigan.

ISBN 1-886472-70-X

Printed in the United States by Publishers Press, Salt Lake City, Utah

Introduction

Being a teenager in high school or a young adult in college can be such a fun time in one's life. I have so many fond memories of the fun I had when I was that age! There was, however, one very important lesson I learned during those years. It was that turning the magic age of "16" does not necessarily mean that boys flock to your house every weekend to ask you out on a date! Shocking but true!

It seems that boys (and now that I have four sons of my own I am even more convinced) have many things to think about…and dating does not seem to rank high on the list! But they do love a party or other fun group activity. So don't just sit around every weekend feeling lonely and thinking your life is dull and uneventful. Instead, gather all your friends together and start making your house or apartment the party place to be! With a little preparation and organization, and with the help of your family and friends, you can create fun times for yourself and others!

The ideas in this book are to help you get your "creative genius" started. You do not have to live in a large city or in an area that provides a lot of entertainment in order to have fun. You can easily create your own!

If you live at home, let your parents and brothers and sisters help with the party preparations. Your parents want to be involved in your life and would love to help you out if they can. Ask your siblings to act as the waiter or waitress during a fun creative meal. This is your chance to let them get a little involved in your life and have some fun too. Not only will everyone have a great time, but you will grow closer to *both* your friends and family.

I am so excited to finally get this book published because I wrote it in hopes of helping *you* create many happy memories in your life! Well, I did my part—now the rest is up to you. So roll up your sleeves, get to work, and have some fun!

Shelley

Table of Contents

Cowpokin' Party

This is your big chance to be a real hick! Whether you're from the West or not, this evening definitely will bring the Wild West to life. Before the kids arrive, string a homemade banner across the front of the house "Welcome to the Watering Hole Saloon and Cafe". Lively country music in the background and western decorations also set the mood. Table decorations might include a checkered tablecloth, bottled root beer, canteens, bandannas for napkins, and an old cowboy boot with flowers for the centerpiece.

As they arrive, give everyone a cowboy hat. You could have everyone bring his or her own, or you can buy them for about $1.20 each from the Oriental Trading Company, Inc. (call 800-228-2269 for a free catalog). Be sure to take a black and white picture of each person or couple--no smiles allowed--and give it to them later as a fun keepsake. Seat everyone at the table and inform them that

"Cowboy Joe" will be their waiter for the evening. Give them the menu, noting that this is a four-course meal, and have them circle which items they would like. Since they don't know exactly what they're choosing, you may get some surprised looks as you bring them their food. The menu is as follows:

Key to Menu

Main Dishes:	Butcher's Special	(Cubed Steak)
	Roped Calf with Cheese	(Cheeseburger)
	Cowboy Slop	(Stew)
	Cluck Bites	(Chicken nuggets)
Side Dishes:	Pitched Hay	(Tossed Green salad)
	Bales of Straw	(Trisket crackers)
	Campfire Tators	(Tator tots or fries)
	Cowboy Vittles	(Pork and beans)
	Ground Kernels	(Biscuits)
	Bunny Sticks	(Carrot sticks)
Drinks:	Cactus Drink	(7 up)
	Guzzle Juice	(Grape or apple juice)
	Belly up to the Bar Special	(Root beer in a bottle)
	Utterly Delightful	(Milk)
Dessert:	Mud Hole	(Frozen chocolate pie)
	Cow Pie Dessert	(Big Wheel ice cream sandwich)
	Bronco bars	(Granola bar)
	Deer Droppings in Snow	(Chocolate chips in ice cream)

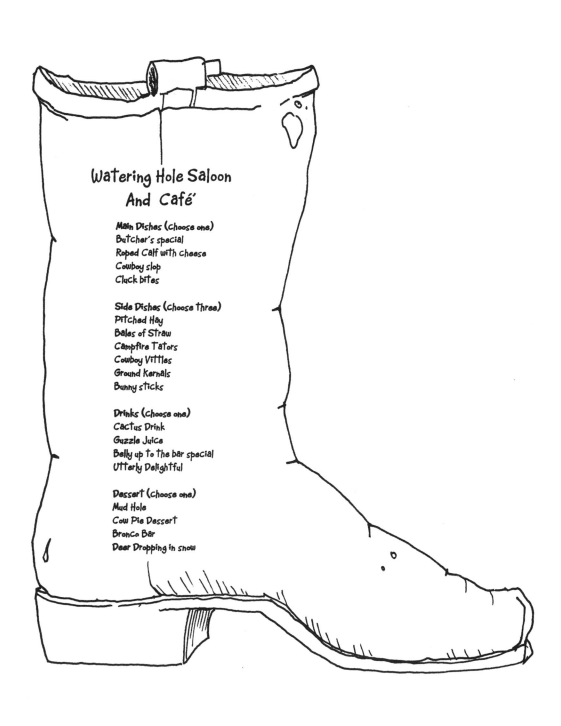

Watering Hole Saloon
And Café

Main Dishes (choose one)
Butcher's special
Roped Calf with cheese
Cowboy slop
Cluck bites

Side Dishes (choose three)
Pitched Hay
Bales of Straw
Campfire Tators
Cowboy Vittles
Ground Kernals
Bunny sticks

Drinks (choose one)
Cactus Drink
Guzzle Juice
Belly up to the bar special
Utterly Delightful

Dessert (choose one)
Mud Hole
Cow Pie Dessert
Bronco Bar
Deer Dropping in snow

After dinner, jump right into the activities. A few suggestions are:

 A Hoe Down

Find someone who can teach square dancing. It's hard not to have fun when you're docido-ing your date. Line dancing can be a real "kick" as well.

Bronco Busting

Find all your old brooms. If you don't have enough, have the kids bring their own horses (brooms) to the party. Mount them up like horses and race them around an obstacle course with old barrels or kitchen chairs!

Hula Hoop Roping Contest

Purchase two small hula hoops and tie a rope on each one. On the count of three, have two guys chase their dates and try to rope them with their hula hoops. After the girls are caught, it's their turn to rope the guys. Make sure everyone gets a turn and afterward, hand out awards!

Chicken Pecking

Fill a child's small swimming pool with about three inches of popcorn and hide several pieces of wrapped candy throughout. On the count of three have each person peck in the popcorn to find the candy. Give them four minutes and the winner is the person who finds the most candy without cheating! Pecking only. No hands allowed.

Chug a Mug Contest

Buy root beer and several 2-liter mugs at your local Walmart. Have two couples at a time race to see who can "chug" the root beer the fastest. Make sure to time each couple and when everyone's done, have the two couples with the best times race again.

Gambling for Dough

Divide into groups of four or six, and play any card game that doesn't take a long time to win (i.e. UNO, Phase 10, etc.). Each time a person wins a round, they get some "dough"--that is, cookie dough. (Prepare in advance by placing a scoop of cookie dough in a baggy and tie a piece of string around it—this "bag of dough" will serve as the reward for the winners.) Then start another round. After a set period of time, the couples combine their dough, bake their dough in the oven, and then share their winnings.

Rodeo Fun

If you live close to a rodeo, it's a great activity full of action and fun.

The 4th or 24th of July are great times to have a Cowpokin' Party because that's when most of the rodeos are happening.

Campfire

You can never go wrong having a campfire. The nice thing is that you can have one outside or even inside by using your fireplace or by making a fake fire. You can make a fake fire by placing large stones in a circle, and putting red, orange, or yellow cellophane between, under, and around a couple of big logs. Place several flashlights under the cellophane and you have a nice looking fire. Telling cowboy stories and roasting marshmallows is a fun way to end the party. Also, make sure to invite someone who can play the guitar and have a sing-a-long.

Search & Scrounge

This is the cheapest date you will ever have! The cost...is free! In fact if you charge an admission fee to come to your party, you might actually make a few cents!

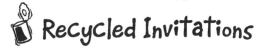

Recycled Invitations

Invite your dates by using crumpled up paper or the back of a returned homework assignment. Take a used envelope, scratch out the name, and re-address it to your guests! Tell everyone to wear old hand-me-downs (the tackier, the better). Or, if you have the time, go with your date to a second-hand store and pick out each other's clothes for the evening for about $3.00 apiece.

"Find the Loot"

When your guests arrive, tell them they must pay an entrance fee of $0.29 to help cover the cost of the party. They need to find four pennies, one nickel, and two dimes. They can either search your house or go to another party guest's house to find it. The rule is that they can't ask anyone for it; they must FIND it. Have them look in the washing machine, under the couch, between the cushions, etc. When they return, collect the money in an old cup to help pay for the party!

"Scrounge Smorgasbord"

Give each person a cleaned out tin can (soup cans work nicely) and a plastic spoon. Let them know you really don't have any money for this party and so they are going to have to scrounge for their dinner. They must go from house to house in search of their meal, asking for leftovers. They can go to friends, neighbors, the bishop, home teachers and seminary teachers, or YM and YW leaders (they will be having just as much fun as you are, so don't be embarrassed). Everyone needs to walk into the house and have a spokesman say, "We are broke! We were wondering if we might possibly have any leftovers you could spare, even just a piece of bread would be nice!" Then let them fill your cans with the food, eat it in front of them, then go to the next house and beg. Do this until you are full!

Freebie Search

Scrounge up a freebie video to watch later in the evening. Borrow it from friends, neighbors, or relatives or get a free video at the library. If you go to your local video store, sometimes they have free videos for kids, give them a sob story about how you don't have any money and were wondering if they had any free videos.

Disposable Volleyball

In the backyard or garage, hang a rope across a playing area. If you have a volleyball stand or can go to a park and use those facilities, all the better! Divide into two teams for a roaring fun garbage volleyball tournament. Let your friends know that you are too poor to buy a real volleyball and so you are going to play with garbage! For the volleyball, use two black plastic bags (one inside the other for reinforcement) filled with wadded up papers or balloons or any other lightweight garbage, and tie it up tight. Same rules apply as for regular volleyball.

Grotesque Snacks

While enjoying the games and video, serve Kool-aid in plastic cups with garbage floating on the top. Sliced carrots and celery or orange and lemon peels work wonderful and will not ruin the taste of the drink. Just before your guests go home, let everyone know that if they are still hungry they will have to "dig through the garbage" for their dessert. Use your garbage can (clean it out first) and then add rolled up newspaper or computer paper (clean garbage) to the can. Purchase several candy bars and break off a piece of the candy bar so that it looks half eaten. **You get to eat what you break off! Yummy!** Then re-wrap it and scatter the remainder of the candy bars throughout.

Strip Poker

Don't worry! It's not as bad as it sounds! This is a conservative, "Mormon" strip poker game that requires toothpicks, Hershey Kisses and two dice. Start by having everyone sit around a table and then empty out a bag or two of Hershey Hugs and/or Kisses in the middle of the table. Next, give each person two toothpicks. Explain that these will act as "poker" sticks. They will be used to unwrap (or, "strip") the Hershey Kisses that are on the table. Action begins as one person starts rolling the dice. They continue doing so until they roll a double. While this person is rolling, the person to his or her right uses the poker sticks to unwrap, or strip, a Hershey Kiss. They try to strip and eat as many Kisses as possible before the person to their left rolls a double. Once the double has been rolled, the person rolling yells "Doubles!" and passes the dice to the person that has just been doing the stripping. This person then begins to roll the dice, attempting to roll doubles, and the person to his right begins stripping kisses using his toothpicks. This process continues around the table until all of the Kisses have been stripped and eaten. Everyone keeps his or her wrappers to count how many kisses he or she has stripped and eaten. The winner receives…five kisses (the candy) but it could be real kisses!

A Touch of Class

It is not often that teens have the money and means for a high-class meal at a high-class restaurant, so this is your chance to impress the girl or guy of your dreams! Tell your dates that you have prepared an unforgettable evening including reservations at the best restaurant in town! Formal wear is required. Prior to the date, have a long stem rose delivered to the door. Ask a parent or friend to act as chauffeur wearing a dark suit, white gloves and a top hat. Drive around town for a while and to their surprise, your final destination will be McDonald's.

Call McDonald's first to ask permission and tell them what you are doing. Have a family member prepare the table before you arrive. Escort your dates to the nicely decorated table, set with crystal and lit by candlelight. Don't forget to have your own personal waiter or waitress on hand to take the orders and get the food from the front counter. This is an example of a possible menu:

Key to Menu:

MAIN COURSE:

Steakette	(Big Mac)
Chicken Delight	(McChicken Sandwich)
Poached Fillet of Sole	(Fish Fillet)
Ground Round Smothered in Sauce	(Quarter Pounder)
AuGratin Puffs	(Fries)

DRINKS:

Chocolate on the Rocks	(Milk shake)
Orange Stinger	(Orange pop)
Cola Screwdriver	(Cola drinks)
Bloody Ronald	(Root beer)

DESSERTS:

Chocolate Parfait	(Chocolate sundae)
Tropical Cup	(Yogurt cup)
Finger Drops	(McDonald's cookies)

During the meal, have a friend serenade you by playing the violin or other musical instrument–even a trumpet would be funny!

Dinner Menu

Main Course:

Steakette
Chicken Delight
Poached Fillet of Sole
Ground Round smothered in sauce
AuGratin Puffs

Drinks:

Chocolate on the rocks
Orange Stinger
Cola Screwdriver
Bloody Ronald

Desserts:

Chocolate Parfait
Tropical Cup
Finger Drops

"Say Cheese"

This is a really fun activity with do-it-yourself backdrops. For your props you will need an old couch that you can throw in the back of a pickup and take to different scenic spots in your area. Take pictures on a street median, a bridge, in a grocery store, on a mountain top, a graveyard, next to a lake or river, or at the dump--use your imagination because each area has its own unique places. In Wyoming we like to take pictures next to a horse corral. After you are done taking your photos, make a quick trip to the WalMart one-hour photo developing counter. Choose your favorite pictures, and have them blown up to any size you want so that you can remember the fun time you had!

Water Follies

Water activities are always sure to be a great success in the summer! Cool down and enjoy a day of water, laughs, and friends! Tell all your guests to bring a swimming suit or shorts and a T-shirt and towel, and warn them that they will be getting wet-- very, very wet!

Squirt Hunt

This game is played throughout the whole party. Each person should bring his own cheap, small squirt gun to the party. But be prepared for those smart alecks that might bring their super-soakers! At any point during the party, any person can go up to another person, point the squirt gun at him, and ask, "What is my name?" The person being asked must be able to say the other person's first, middle, and last name by the time the person counts to five. If he can't say it fast enough, he is squirted in the face. Then he places his gun back into his pocket until the next time he draws it on somebody!

Splash Parachute

Fill up several large water balloons. Divide the group into two teams and give each team a large blanket. Place one balloon in the center of each blanket and have the team count how many times they can toss the balloon up without breaking it. The balloon must be tossed at least ten feet off the blanket. They must count as they go, and the winning team is the one that gets the highest number.

Seed Spitting

Cut open a large watermelon and divide the group into two teams. Give each team member a small paper cup (Dixie cups work the best). Each person is to eat a slice of watermelon, spitting the seeds into their individual cup as they do. They then transfer all their seeds to the team cup. Continue eating slices of watermelon until it is all gone. The team with the most seeds is the winner. Award the winning team members with watermelon gum.

Water on a Stick Race

Have a race to see who can eat a Popsicle the fastest.

Bombs Away

Have everyone grab a partner and stand across from each other in two straight lines. Give each person on one side a water balloon and on the count of three have them toss the water balloon to their partner. If they catch it, they must take a step back and toss it back to their partner. Continue tossing and moving further away from each other until the balloon breaks. The winners are the last ones to break their balloon.

JELL-O Slurping Contest

Make several packages of JELL-O, following the instructions on the package except adding an extra half-cup of the water. This makes the JELL-O less firm than normal. (For example, add 2 ½ cups water to a small package of JELL-O.) If it is too firm, don't worry. Simply stir in some water just before the contest! Fill paper cups with equal portions of the JELL-O, and give one of these cups and a straw to each person. Using the straw, and on the command of "GO", the first person to successfully slurp up the entire paper cup of gelatin is the winner!

Water Volleyball

Set up a volleyball net in your yard or, if not readily available, simply tie a rope between the house and a tree. In advance, fill at least four or five dozen water balloons. The bigger the balloons and the fuller you fill them, the more fun it is! Place the water balloons near the playing area. Divide into two teams, with the teams positioned on opposite sides of the net, similar to regular volleyball. Each team member should have a partner with whom he or she shares a bath towel. The towel is stretched out between them, each person holding onto two of the corners.

Using the towel, each pair of players works as a team, serving, catching, and tossing the water balloon over the net. If the balloon is missed and breaks, the team that tossed it over the net gets the point and the next serve. It will take a few warm-up tosses and catches to become proficient at this, but everyone should catch on quickly!

Sponge Ball Frenzy

Divide the group into two equal teams and have them get into two straight lines with a bucket of water on each end of the lines. On the count of "one-two-three-GO", the two individuals at the beginning of each line dip a sponge ball into the water, place it between their neck and chin, and then pass it to the next person without using their hands (passing it from neck to neck). Each team passes the wet sponge ball down the line until it gets to the last person. The last person then grabs the ball from under his chin, dips it in the bucket of water next to him, places it again under his chin, and starts the ball going back up the line. The first team to get the sponge ball back to the beginning wins. It's fun to play this game several times.

Musical Tidal Wave

Have everyone sit in a circle around a small, children's swimming pool full of water. Turn on lively music and begin passing a large bucket from one person to the next around the circle. When the music stops, the person holding the bucket fills it with water from the swimming pool, yells "Tidal Wave", and dumps or throws the bucket of water all over whoever he chooses. Then, start the music again and continue passing the bucket around the circle until the music stops. Continue in this manner until everyone is soaked!

Ice Sliding

Buy big, solid ice blocks from your local grocery store. Then find a good-sized hill and slide down on the ice blocks with an old towel on top to help you stay on.

Frozen Finger Melt Down

Give each person an ice cube. The first one to melt his or her ice cube (without putting it in their mouth) is the winner.

Let the Good Times Roll!

It's always fun to look back to the past and relive an era--and the 50's was such a great time in history, filled with great music, great clothes, and great food! Have everyone dress in 50's apparel. Guys can slick back their hair and wear rolled-up jeans and white T-shirts. Girls can wear poodle skirts, white bobby socks, a sweater with the arms tied around their neck and hair in ponytails or pigtails. Get out your parent's old rock 'n roll music, making sure it's the good bebop music! Have each person bring pennies for the diner.

Penny's Diner

Pick up your dates with 50's music playing in your car. Hang a homemade banner across your garage saying "Penny's Drive Inn and Diner." Have 50's music blaring in the background. As you pull up in the driveway, park your car and wait for the hops that are all dressed up in poodle skirts, pig tails, and knee high socks. Have them come gliding up to the car wearing their roller skates. (This is a great time to use your younger brothers or sisters who are not old enough to date themselves—they make great car hops!) Make up a menu of greasy hamburgers, cheeseburgers, fries, and thick malts. Have the hops take the order and skate back in the house, where Mom and Dad are working inside the "Diner" as cooks. It works best if you have two carloads of kids. Of course, you are going to have to pay the car hops a good tip (your younger brothers and sisters won't think it is fun if you don't), so…charge everyone a penny!

 # Drive In Movie

After dinner, drive around the block and come back and park in the garage for a drive-inn movie. Beforehand, have the TV, VCR, and "snack bar" set up on a table or workbench in the garage. Post a sign that gives the costs of the snacks. Everything under a dime of course! The snack bar can include large dill pickles, candy bars, popcorn, and soda pop. Turn off the car and unroll the window so you don't fog up. Rent a 50's video like **Bye Bye Birdie**, the **Pajama Game**, or any great sci-fi flick. No necking please!

Brylcream Contest

This is a chance for you to demonstrate your wonderful talent in hairdressing, or if you hate your date's style, here is a chance for you to change it!

Instead of actually using Brylcream, since it is expensive and hard to wash out, use shaving cream or thick styling gel and see who can make the wildest looking 'do.

Soda Pop Sipping Contest

Give each couple a pitcher containing about two liters of soda pop and two straws. The couple who sips all of the pop first, wins.

Bubble Gum Contest

During the 50's bubble gum was the "in" thing, so give everyone at least two pieces of bubble gum and have a bubble gum blowing contest. Give awards for those who make the biggest, loudest, smallest, and messiest bubbles.

Frightening Film Festival

Instead of just having friends over to watch a scary movie, try calling the evening a "Frightening Film Festival." If you call it that, your friends will come prepared for a great time and be ready for a good scare, too! Plus, if you want to get close to your honey, a scary movie will do it every time! Turn off the lights and enjoy a night of fright.

A few really good and scary movies include **Wait Until Dark, Lady in White, Fall of the House of Usher, Watcher in the Woods, The Raven,** or the old versions of **The Haunting,** and **Psycho**. During the scariest part, have a younger sibling come in and scare someone! Ha! Ha! After the movie, while everyone is a bit shaky, move right into the activities. Some suggestions are:

Hide and Scare

This is a great game that is guaranteed to make you jump! It is similar to flashlight hide-and-go-seek except that you are in couples. One couple is "it" and searches for the other couples who are hiding. Everyone who is hiding tries to scare the "it" couple before they get caught. If the "it" couple sees them, shines their flashlight on them, and shouts out their name, they are out. However, if a hiding couple scares the "it" couple before they get caught, the "it" couple must close their eyes for 20 seconds to allow them to hide again. The couple who is found last wins.

Spooky Search

This is a fun activity to do in a large building or a big house, or in a park with a lot of trees. It must be completely dark when playing this game. Have everyone meet in a room and have one person leave and go hide. Then, with scary music playing in the background, everyone must exit the room and quietly go and find the person who is hiding. When anyone finds this person, he or she must sit down quietly next to him. As others find them, they quietly do the same. The last person to find the hidden group is the next person to go hide during the next round of the game.

💀 Grave Diggers Hunt

Go to the local graveyard. It might be more fun and less trouble to find an old deserted graveyard, but if not, be sure to ask permission to go there after dark. (You might have better luck if you tell them that a parent will go along to act as a chaperon). Divide the group into couples and give each couple four names that they need to find. You have previously been to the graveyard and have taken down names and death dates off the tombstones. Give them each a flashlight, and a tablet, and a pen and have them go two by two into the graveyard to search for the names. They must prove they have found the graves by putting down the death dates.

💀 Tombstone Ice Cream

Purchase a half-gallon of your favorite flavored ice cream. Completely unwrap the ice cream from its carton. Slice the ice cream into rectangular blocks, each block large enough to serve one person. Place the blocks of ice cream on a serving tray, one block for each guest. Crush a bag of Oreo cookies using a rolling pin. This will become your "dirt." Place this "dirt" over each block of ice cream, pressing gently into the ice cream by using your hands. Now you have made a "grave" for each person. Using white poster board cut out a small tombstone. On the tombstone, use black magic marker to write "R.I.P." (which means, "Rest in Peace") and under this write a person's name. Cut out and mark a tombstone for each person. By gently pressing, attach one of these tombstones onto the end of each grave. Place the serving tray in the freezer until dessert time, and then present each person with his or her own personalized "grave."

Pajama Party

Inform everyone that you are having a pajama party. Have your friends come in modest pajamas that can be worn in public, and have them bring their favorite stuffed animal and pillow!

 ## Cartoon Madness

Begin the evening by watching rented cartoon videos. Tiny Toons and Looney Toons, and any Pinkie and the Brain cartoons are fun to watch and are actually pretty funny! Buy an assortment of "high sugar cereals" and put them in bowls (like eating popcorn) for everyone to snack on during the movie!

Sleeping Bag Relay

Unroll two sleeping bags and place them on the ground. Divide into two teams and get ready to start the race. Use the sleeping bags like gunnysacks, hopping down to a pre-determined line and back again and then pass the bag to the next team member in line.

 # Sock Pull

To play this, have everyone take off their shoes and get on their hands and knees on the living room floor. On "GO" each person tries to pull the socks off everyone else while keeping their own socks on. No kicking allowed, no sitting on your feet, and stay on your knees at all times. When you lose both of your socks you are out of the game and move off to the side to watch. This is a fun game to do several times!

 # Pancake Eating Contest

Seat everyone at a large table with a heaping plate of pancakes. Cheap pancake mix that only needs water is the best. Each person takes one pancake, puts on a topping, and eats it completely. They do not get another pancake to eat until everyone has finished theirs. Continue each round and keep track of how many rounds they have had. The winner is the person who eats the most pancakes.

Before Bedtime Frenzy

This is a progressive bedtime hunt. The following things must be done before you can have…a pillow fight. Split into two groups and send the following list with each group. Make sure to leave room on the list for signatures of witnesses. Winners are the team members who come back first and who have completed the hunt!

1. Have a gargling contest. (See who can gargle "Scope" or another brand of mouthwash the longest.)
2. Go to a dentist's house and have your teeth checked to make sure they are clean enough to go to bed. If you don't personally know a dentist, how about a hygienist, or an orthodontist?
3. Have a mother (any mother) read you a bedtime story.
4. Go to the bathroom at someone in your group's house. Everyone must individually walk into the bathroom, flush the toilet, and save a piece of toilet paper as evidence.
5. Go to someone in your group's house and find a bedtime snack.
6. Go find someone who plays a musical instrument and have him·or her play a goodnight lullaby to you.
7. Get a goodnight kiss from someone. If it becomes difficult, you can always pay someone…for a kiss goodnight.

Have a pillow fight—it can be done in rounds. It works best to have girls against girls and boys against boys. Have the people in the first round grab their pillows and attack each other for two minutes. Then, it's the second group's turn. Set some rules so that no one gets hurt…especially the girls!

An Evening in Mexico

Uno, dos, tres, your house will be the party place! I know that all of you have had some Spanish in high school or middle school! This is your chance to use that Spanish... at least you can say a few words...can't you? When your guests arrive, seat them at a table where there are Mexican hats for each person. (You can purchase these hats through a local party store or very inexpensively through mail order from Oriental Trading Company (1-800–228-2269). Upbeat Mexican music in the background also adds to the fun. Take advantage of your local library and check out some music from there.

Dress a younger sibling or friend as a Mexican waitress and call him or her Juanita. A black wig with a flower in her or his ear, and a wonderful Mexican-like dress can be found pretty easily at a second-hand store. She takes orders and gives everyone several choices of Mexican dishes. Some possible ideas for food could

29

be taco salad, enchiladas, chips with salsa, quesadillas. After dinner, jump right into the activities. Some may include:

 ## Mexican Flip Dip

Divide the group into pairs giving each person a small bowl full of Mexican dip. You can use a guacamole dip, or sour cream, or even heat up some refried beans. Each person will also need a plastic spoon. Have the couples sit facing each other a few feet apart. They must then empty their bowl of dip by flipping the dip into his or her partner's mouth.

 ## Limbo

The key to having a fun limbo contest is having great music playing in the background. While two people hold a broom, a rope, or bamboo stick about chest high, have everyone else line up and take turns attempting to go under the stick. They must lean back and walk straight under it (no bending forward or sideways) without touching the stick with any part of their body. If they touch it, then they are out of the game and must watch. When everyone has had a turn, lower the rope or stick a few inches and everyone who is still in goes under it again. The winner is the last one to successfully go under the rope or stick.

 ## Tequila Drinking Contest

Pass out old-fashioned bottles of root beer and have each person place a gummy worm in their bottle. Explain that in Mexico, tequila is made from cactus and that they usually drink it with a cactus worm in it. On the count of three have three or four people at a time see how fast they can "chug" their drink. The winner is the person that drinks all of it and grabs the gummy worm between their teeth. Time each person and after everyone has had a turn, have the two fastest race again.

 "Fire Tongue"

Prepare several hard shell tacos. Use a whole bottle of hot Tabasco sauce in the ground beef used to make the taco. Get the guys to volunteer and put about three tacos and a glass of water in front of them on the table. At the word go they have to finish all the tacos and drink the water. The winner gets the leftover bottle of hot sauce for a memento!

Piñata

Breaking a piñata is an excellent way to end the evening, and a perfect way to eat dessert. Fill the piñata with plenty of wrapped candy and hang it from a tree or swing set or other safe place. After blindfolding a person, spin them around and give them a bat. Each person can have three swings, and when it is finally broken and all the candy has fallen out, everyone can scramble for the goods inside!

Video

A great video to watch for a Mexican Fiesta is **The Three Amigos** (PG) starring Chevy Chase, Steve Martin, and Martin Short.

Beat the Heat

I know you have heard the phrase: "The grass is always greener on the other side of the fence." That basically means we are never happy or satisfied with what we have! It seems like that's the case with most things in life. For example, sometimes on a hot, sunny day we wish it were winter. This is a fun party that combines the best of both seasons and you don't have to worry about being snowed in! Have the group come dressed in their winter wear--hats, gloves, jackets, and snow boots!

❄ Snowball Eating Contest

This is a great eating contest involving powdered sugar donut holes. Or, if you can find them at your local grocery store, Hostess "Snowballs" will do the trick. Have four or five volunteers sit at a table that has a big pile of donut holes or "Snowballs" in front of them. Give them one minute to see how many snowballs they can eat, with the other guests keeping track. The winner gets to kiss whoever they want on the cheek with their powdery lips! (Tell them this before they start, it gives them an even greater incentive to win!)

❄Snowball Fight

Divide the "battleground" with a rope and get into two teams. Give each team several bags of marshmallows, or wadded up paper balls, and have them throw the "snowballs" at each other. They must stay on their side of the line, trying to keep as many snowballs as they can off their side and get as many on the opposing side as possible. Let them do this for five minutes and then count and see who has the most snowballs on their side.

❄The Great Skate

A few days before the party make homemade ice skates by freezing water in bread pans. Lay two shoelaces widthwise in the water, so that they are frozen into the ice block. Use the shoelaces to tie the ice blocks onto their shoes. Make a fun course for them to follow. The first player to cross the finish line wins.

❄Snow Feeding Contest

Divide into couples and give each couple a can of whipped cream—the kind that you can squirt out of the nozzle. In this race the couples take turns spraying whipped cream into their partner's mouth. The winner is the couple that finished eating all the whipped cream the fastest.

❄ Cold Snow Plop

This is an extremely messy activity so have the participants wear old T-shirts or plastic garbage bags over their clothes. Split into couples and have about two couples go at a time. One person lies on the ground with their head near a chair, and their partner stands on the chair while holding a spoon and a bowl of ice cream. The object is to try to get the ice cream into the mouth of the person lying down by dropping spoonfuls of ice cream from above. The person standing on the chair must drop the ice cream from their spoon held about waist high. No fair bending over to get closer. When the person lying down has finished the bowl of ice cream, he or she switches places with the person on the chair. Now it's their chance to turn their partner's face into an ice cream mountain!

❄ Snowball Express

A great video to watch for the winter in summer party is Walt Disney's **SnowBall Express.**

Toddling Back into Time

Dressing and acting like a baby may sound ridiculous, but it's fun being a little immature at times! In order to come to your party, guests must come dressed as babies or toddlers. Sheets or dishtowels can be used as diapers. Bib overalls, shorts and knee socks, freckles drawn on your face, rosy cheeks, baseball caps worn backwards, pigtails, etc., are the styles!

Give each "baby" a candy pacifier–it is actually called a ring pop and can be purchased at dime store. Attach a piece of string or yarn around each pacifier. Some of the activities may include:

Baby Bottle Drinking and Belching Contest

Divide into couples and have two couples race against each other. Give each couple a baby bottle (run a hot needle through the hole in the nipple so that it's a little bigger than normal) and have them feed their partners the bottle, sitting on his or her lap. They must drink the whole bottle and then burp! Pop works the best because the carbonation makes it easy to burp up!

Baby Wipe out Tournament

Purchase two containers of baby wipes—the kind that can be pulled out from the top. This is a fun relay. You divide into two teams and place the two containers of baby wipes about fifteen feet in front of the contestants. On the count of three, the first person on each team runs and grabs a baby wipe, and runs back and tags the next person in line. If the wipes don't come out, then they'll have to take the top off the container and thread the wipes back through the hole. Keep going until all the baby wipes are gone.

Jump Rope Mania

Use a large rope and take turns jumping or turning the rope. Have the group jump to the rhymes they learned during first grade recess. For example: "Tom and Susie, sitting in a tree. K-I-S-S-I-N-G. First comes love, then comes marriage. Then comes Susie with a baby carriage!" Others might include, "Texaco, Texaco, over the hill to Mexico." If you have forgotten some of the fun jump rope rhymes, check with your younger siblings for ideas.

🎀 Finger Paint with Pudding

Roll out butcher paper, newspaper ends, or freezer wrap on the dining room table or kitchen bar. (You can often purchase newspaper ends at the business office of your local community newspaper.) Bring out finger paint that you purchased, or make your own homemade finger-paint by making up pudding. Danish Delight, banana, chocolate, and pistachio puddings work great! This way you can paint a little, eat a little, paint a little!

🎀 Snack Time

Everyone loves snack time! McDonald's has fun baby bibs that are free and they seem happy to give away. Ask for enough to give one to each baby coming to your party. Purchase animal crackers, or teddy graham cookies. Don't forget the bottled baby food too! Check with some of the younger families in your ward or neighborhood and see if they have empty baby food bottles. Fill the bottles with your mom's good "homemade" applesauce.

🎀 Story Time

This is a real favorite. Have everyone sit in a circle while someone, acting as a mommy or daddy, reads wonderful stories to them. Dr. Suess books are some of the best, or find some of your favorite books that your mommy used to read to you!

✿ Music Time

Put on some great classical or children's music. Give the children or babies a five-foot piece of crepe paper and have them dance with the crepe paper twirling around them, getting a real "feel" for the music!

✿ Edible Challenge

Buy a variety of Gerber baby food jars. Asparagus, peas, carrots, peaches and cream, and chicken dinner are a few good choices. Take off the labels of the baby food, then allow everyone to taste the contents of each jar and guess it's flavor. The winner is the one who gets the most right.

✿ Baby Relay

Gather and find several items for this fun relay. Possible items might include two wagons, two big wheels, or two scooters. You will also need a couple of stools to act as high chairs. Divide into two teams and set the high chairs about 20 feet away from the starting line. The first two contestants in line must work together. One baby must ride in the wagon, the other baby pulling, to the high chair, put on a bib and while sitting in the high chair must be fed a bottle of baby food, then they must jump on the big wheel or scooter and ride back to the line. This continues until all babies have participated.

Crazy Car Rally

Driving in a road rally can be disastrous for teens! You will be having so much fun that you may forget all about "stop signs," "speed limits," and "signaling"! My advice…ask your parents to drive so that you can relax and have fun, too!

Divide your guests into teams of about four or five people per car. Give each team a large paper sack with the following inside: sandwich bags, sufficient money to purchase or to do all of the items on the road rally list, a rag to dry the car after it is washed, and a pen or a pencil. Write up a list of approximately 15 items that each team must accomplish. Both teams get the same list, but one team will start with item #1 on the list while the other team begins with item #7 (so that you both aren't traveling to the same places at the same time).

All activities must be completed in the order in which they are listed. Two items on the list cannot be accomplished at the same place. Each stop will need a signature or some kind of proof that it was completed. All items on the list must be accomplished before a team can head for the pre-determined finish line. Following are some examples of the type of items that you might include on your road rally list:

1. Go to a grocery store and purchase an orange and have the cashier autograph the orange.

2. Go to a local restaurant and get the prices for a taco, a bean burrito, two enchiladas and a chimichonga. Have an employee write down the prices on the restaurant bag or napkin.

3. Go to someone's house in your group and ask for their leftovers from dinner that night and put it in a small container or sandwich bag to eat later.

4. Buy an order of french-fries and save one fry and a package of catsup.

5. Find a park with lots of playground equipment. Each team member must try out each piece of equipment. Then have everyone in the group climb a tree and have someone who saw you sign here. _____

6. Buy a loaf of bread. Everyone must take a bite out of the center of their own slice. Add this to your collection of evidence.

7. Find a bagger at a grocery store who has curly hair and have him or her sign here: _____

8. Thirsty? Buy a milk shake at a fast food restaurant and share it with everyone. Keep all of the straws as evidence.

9. Go to a drive up window at a local fast food restaurant. Purchase a hamburger. Let everyone have a bite. Save the pickle and drop it in your bag.

10. Find an out-of-state car and write down the license number here: _____

11. Find a gum ball machine and buy enough gum for each person to have six pieces. Have each person chew up their gum and then combine everyone's together to form a gum mountain as proof.

12. Go to someone's home and borrow something from him or her. Place it in your bag.

13. Find a copy machine and make a copy of one team member's hand. Keep a copy!

14. Go to a car wash and clean your car. Don't forget to dry it good! Evidence is the wet towel.

15. Go to the gas station and put fifty-cents of gasoline in your car. Don't forget to get a receipt.

Have refreshments waiting at the pre-determined final destination. These might include donuts (wheels) and black currant juice or root beer (motor oil). Go through each group's list and check to make sure they have all the evidence. The winners are the ones who get back first with everything completed.

Fun at the Mall

Teens love hanging out at the mall, but instead of just "hanging out", think of a mall as a great place to have a date or party! Also, while there you can always look around and make a mental note of items you would like to purchase some other time!

SALE Mall Tag

Start in the center of the mall. Choose one person to be "it" and give the group about one minute to disappear. They don't actually hide, but just wander from store to store trying not to be seen. (No fair hiding in dressing rooms, etc.)

Once seen, that person also becomes "it" and helps to find other members of the group. Those that are found must stay together and search a store or area of the mall as a group. At this point those who have not yet been caught are not sure who has been caught and who hasn't, so they must watch out and try to keep from being spotted by anyone else! Once everyone has been spotted the game is over. (You may want to set a time limit in case one person is especially elusive, every one meeting back at a designated spot at a certain time).

SALE Mall Meal

Purchase a Happy Meal at McDonald's or a Kid's Meal at Burger King, one for each person, set up a blanket in the center of the mall, having a fun picnic on the ground.

SALE The 2 Buck Shopping Spree

Give everyone $2 to go shopping--remember that toy stores have some great stuff! Each person is to purchase things that you can all play with! Some suggestions are jacks, jump rope, bubbles, pick up sticks, etc. Some people might combine their money and buy a more expensive thing. Then play with the toys you have bought on the floor in the mall.

SALE Shopping Mall Derby

The great thing about a busy mall is that there are such a large variety of people. Split up into teams of three or four and have them find people with the following description and get their signatures. The first team with all the signatures wins.

1. Someone who wears a size 11 shoe_____

2. A mother with a baby in a stroller_____

3. A child eating something_____

4. A mother with more than four children_____

5. A teenager buying a CD_____

6. A man wearing ball cap _____

7. A person drinking a drink_____

8. Someone in the restroom_____

9. Someone stocking shelves in a store_____

10. A person using a cart_____

11. A sales clerk in a store_____

12. Someone who is buying something from a vending machine (gumball or candy)_____

13. A man sitting on a bench waiting for his wife_____

Goof Ball Basketball

This is a fun way to spend the evening playing a little basketball! Find a gym to use during the winter months or play at an outside park that has hoops! Warn your friends that the evening has a little twist! The boys must play against the girls... dressed in nylons, dresses, high heels, and stuff they can borrow from their moms and sisters. The girls wear jeans, T-shirts, and sports shoes! Then split the teams, boys versus girls, and have a ball!

Serve hot dogs, chips, and pop on the sideline! Don't forget the video camera!

Going Bananas

This is a great party to have when bananas go on sale at four pounds for a dollar, and it's easy to throw together...all you need is bananas! Tell your guests that they must dress in yellow for this party. Begin the party with dinner and then a series of contests and keep track of the winners.

🍌 Banana Meal

It's not often that you have a meal fixed completely with bananas as a main ingredient. Here is your chance to be very creative in the kitchen. Divide the group into teams of two. Give each team an assignment: a banana "smoothy" drink, a banana pizza or casserole, banana bread, a banana fruit salad, and a desert (banana pudding or cream pie). Hopefully you will have all the ingredients and recipes that your guests will need. Then following the preparation, set the table with yellow paper plates and cups and have fun eating your banana meal!

 # Banana Chop

Seat six or seven people at a table and have them race to see who can chop up a banana into 15 pieces the fastest. Count each piece to make sure they have the exact amount.

 # Speedy Banana Contests

See who can eat the most bananas in three minutes; who can eat a banana the fastest; who can peel a banana the fastest; and who can take the largest bite out of a banana.

 # Banana Cream Pie Contest

Purchase several tin pie pans and fill them with banana cream pudding. Top the pies off with whipped cream. Line up the contestants and give them each a pie. On the count of three, have them race to see who can eat his or her banana pie the fastest. No hands please!

Banana Relay

Divide into two equal teams and give each team a banana. Have the first person on each team hold the banana between their knees and on the count of three, hop to a designated line and back again. They then pass the banana to the next person, and so forth until everyone has gone. The winners get back to the start first. Another fun activity is bobbing for bananas! (Of course, bananas don't float which makes this even more fun!)

Banana Hunt

Go to a local grocery store or WalMart and divide into an even number of teams (two, four, or six teams). Each team has ten minutes to find fifteen yellow items to put into their grocery cart. When their time is up, have the teams return to a pre-determined place and have them switch carts with another team. Then race to see who can put back the fifteen yellow items the fastest.

Steal the Banana

Playing "steal the banana" is similar to playing "steal the flag", except that you use a banana instead of a flag. It's a fun night game!

Giant Banana Split

Purchase a plastic rain gutter from a hardware or building supply store. Cut it to the length of your dining room table and place banana slices along the bottom of the gutter. Next add scoops of your favorite ice cream. If you'd like, add chopped nuts, whipped cream, and cherries. Finish it off by spreading your favorite flavored toppings over the ice cream. Arm everyone with a spoon and dig in!

 ## Golden Banana Awards

Before the party, determine how many winners you plan to have from the various contests. Then, on newspaper, spray bananas with golden spray paint. These make great awards and should be presented to the winners after all the contests.

A Banana Video

If you have time at the end of the party, watch the video **Herbie Goes Bananas.** This is a cute Walt Disney film and a great way to end a fun evening!

Kidnapping Kaper

Wanting a night full of excitement and spontaneity? This is a great way to gather a lot of people to your party without having to formally invite them. Begin this evening by inviting two people of the same sex to your party but don't tell them what they'll be doing. When they arrive, tell them you want them to "kidnap" two others of the opposite sex of their choice to the party. Give them blindfolds and rope. Have them decide who their victims will be, go to their houses and "kidnap" them.

Then have these two who have just been kidnapped, kidnap two more individuals of the opposite sex. Continue until you have the size of party you want and then plan fun activities and enjoy the evening.

Come as You Are

This is a great way to really get to know people in unusual circumstances. First, contact the parents of the individuals you want to come to your early-morning breakfast. Warn them that you want to "kidnap" their son or daughter for the morning and ask them to make sure they are wearing appropriate sleepers. Early the next morning, go around to each person's house, kidnap him or her, and then take them out for breakfast—or, make the breakfast yourself at your house. After breakfast, exercise to an aerobics video or go to your local recreation center for a great workout.

U-Haul Progressive Dinner

A great activity, and one that will be remembered for a long time, is renting a U-Haul truck and planning the activity around it. A small U-Haul truck runs about $19.95 for an evening. It also requires a credit card or deposit (so don't wreck the truck!). Ask your dad or mom to act as a chauffeur. Have them dress the part: wearing a dark suit, a top hat, and white gloves. It might also be fun for everyone on the date to dress in formal wear too!

Then pick up your dates in the U-Haul that you have equipped with a table and chairs. Use your imagination and decorate the inside fancy to impress your dates! Some possible ideas might include: stars covered with tin foil on the ceiling, battery operated candles on the table, a table setting of your mom's best dinnerware (but hang on to it while the truck is in motion), and a fancy tablecloth.

Go from one fast food restaurant to another and at each place have a different course. For example, you may go to Wendy's to get an appetizer like a salad, to Burger King to get dessert, to McDonald's for a drink, etc. At each fast food restaurant have the chauffeur open the back door of the truck for you and then hold open the restaurant door as you escort your dates into the building. Have him stand by the truck until you return. He can then help you back in, close down the door, and then drive to the next stop while you eat and visit.

Bike-a-Meal

Prepare a fun picnic for your friends—something as easy as submarine sandwiches, chips and a dip, finger food tray of veggies and fruit, and an easy dessert. Warn them that they must go on a treasure hunt on their bikes in order to eat!

About an hour before their bike ride, hide the five different food items noted above and the clues that will be used to find them. Conceal them very well so that others who are NOT INVITED will not find and steal your meal! Use a friend's mailbox, a flowerbed at a church, the limb of a tree, a friend's backyard, etc.

Jump on your bicycles and follow the clues, placing the found items in a backpack. Hide the last item at the picnic site where you want to end your journey. Throw a blanket or tablecloth on the ground and you are finally ready to eat! Have some park games ready to play afterwards.

Float & Bloat

    This is a fun day activity for those that live near a river. Have everyone bring an inner-tube to float on, pack a few fun snacks, or possibly lunch in backpacks. Don't forget the lifejackets if the water is deep. Then just lazily float the river and bloat up on the food you brought along! One bit of advice, eat the food right at the start, because there is always a smart aleck in the group who will splash and soak the food. Half the fun is bloating on the food, and no one likes soggy potato chips!

Summer Frolics

Winter can be such a blah time of year, but if you spice it up with a fun "Summer Party," it will make the winter months more bearable and exciting! Have your guests dress in summer wear, and bring a towel--or wear sunglasses, thongs or sandals. Put on some Beach Boys music (can obtain from the library), set up some lawn chairs in the living room, put up a "Palm Beach" sign, and turn the thermostat up high so that it's nice and toasty! Place a small pool in the middle of the room and "carefully" add just an inch or two of water, enough for everyone to take off their shoes and soak their "hot" feet in the cool, clear water. Set up some lawn chairs around the pool and drink cool lemonade with straws while waiting for all your guests to arrive.

 ## A Summer Barbecue

Drag out the barbecue grill from the garage, or if you don't have one and can borrow one from a friend then do it! Grill hamburgers and hot dogs out on the deck and have potato salad, chips and dip. Set up your cooler as part of the decorations and let everyone reach in and grab their own soda pop out. Or, improvise and set up a hot dog stand, where hot dogs and chips can be obtained. Prepare Kool-Aid or soft drinks, placing a slice of orange on the rim of the glass, and stabbing the orange slice with a miniature paper umbrella (which can be found at a party shop)! For a fun summer dessert, purchase small, inexpensive gold fish bowls at your local discount store. Stir and pour blue JELL-O into them, dropping in a few gummy fish for good measure. Give each couple a plastic spoon and a gold fish bowl to share and let them dig in!

 ## Beach Ball Volleyball

Stretch yarn or rope across the living room and attach it to opposite walls about five feet off the ground. Divide into two teams and play using regular volleyball rules, but use a balloon or beach ball instead.

Winter Tan Contest

After a long time without exposure to the sun, skin has a tendency to lose its nice tan. Have everyone roll up their pant legs to show off their white legs. The whitest legs win the contest. The winner gets a bottle of suntan lotion.

 # Ice Cube Melting Contest

Give each person an ice cube and have a race to see who can melt their ice cube the fastest. No fair placing it in your mouth!

 # Limbo

The key to having a fun limbo contest is having great music playing in the background. While two people hold a broom, a rope, or bamboo stick about chest high, have everyone else line up and take turns attempting to go under the stick. They must lean back and walk straight under it (no bending forward or sideways) without touching the stick with any part of their body. If they touch it, then they are out of the game and must watch. When everyone has had a turn, lower the rope or stick a few inches and everyone who is still in goes under it again. The winner is the last one to successfully go under the rope or stick.

 # Cold Drop

One member of each team lies on the ground with a towel under his head while another team member stands on a chair next to him. The person on the chair holds a bowl of ice cream and a large spoon in his hands about waist high. On "GO" each person standing on a chair attempts to drop a scoop of ice cream directly into his team member's mouth. Team members can take turns standing on the chair and dropping the ice cream. The team to get the most ice cream in their team member's mouth wins!

 ## Beach Ball Blow

Purchase beach balls (can order through Oriental Trading Company for about $6.00 a dozen or at any party shop), and give each person their own. See who can blow up their ball the fastest. This is a fun activity because beach balls are not that easy to blow up!

 ## Sand Castles

Make your own play dough or purchase some in small cans at WalMart or other discount stores. Give everyone a blob or a can of play dough and have them make and design their own unique sandcastle. Decide whose castle looks the best!

In the Army

Tell your guests to come in their khaki pants (green or brown). If they like, they can darken their skin with eye shadow in order to look camouflaged. When they arrive, give them each recruiting forms to fill out.

Hand each person a dog tag. You can order these from Oriental Trading Company for $2.40 a dozen, or make your own out of thick gray card stock. Attach some string so they can hang them around their necks. Perhaps your dad can act as the Drill Sergeant and welcome them to boot camp!

 ## Army Attire

Now it's time to have them make their own camouflaged shirt. Give each of your recruits a plain white, cheap T-shirt to tie-dye. You can purchase tie-dye kits, but it is less expensive to just buy some Rit Liquid dye and make your own product. You will need some large buckets, several colors of Rit dye, boiling hot water, salt, and some rubber bands. Fill the large buckets about ¾ full of hot water. Add to it a half-cup of salt and half a bottle of Rit dye, then stir with a large stick. Great colors to use for army attire are black, brown, dark green and gray. Have each person get his or her T-shirt wet. Once it is wrung out, gather the cloth together and shape it into a ball. Wrap rubber bands in a haphazard fashion, keeping the shirt in a round shape. Then dip the shirts into the buckets of dye, either using all one color or several colors. After the shirts are dyed, lay them out on a fence or swing set to dry.

 ## Mess Hall Fun

Check with your parents to see if you can use the dishes from the family camping mess kit. If you don't have any, go to WalMart and pick up some cheap tin plates in the camping or hunting department of the store. Prepare a mess hall meal. Actually, any type of food will work, but don't forget the beans, or possibly use stew that you can slop on their plates!

 ## Obstacle Course

This activity consists of a three-part obstacle course that should take place outside.

Obstacle Course Number 1:

For the first course, take the recruits outside and blindfold each one. One person will act as the leader and will give directions to everyone. You will also need a person to act as a tormentor whose job is to tickle and harass the recruits while on their journey. Instruct each recruit to form a chain, holding onto the waist of the person in front of them. The leader stands at the head of the chain and leads the blind-folded recruits around trees, under swings, over sandboxes, and so forth. The more difficult the course the better.

They must keep holding on to each other and not let go or some may break off from the chain and become lost. The leader should be silent, but the first recruit in line can warn the others behind of obstacles to avoid. They must work together in order to arrive safely at their final destination!

Obstacle Course Number 2:

Prepare the second part of the obstacle course by criss-crossing a long clothesline rope or yarn back-and-forth and up-and-down between two trees or poles of a swing set in order to form a giant spider web. The openings in the web must be large enough so that a person can fit through them. There must be more openings in the web than there are members of the group. The object is to have all members pass through the web without touching the rope. When one member passes through an opening, close off the opening by using a clothespin to attach a file card that states "closed"--it cannot be passed through again.

Members will need to work as a team to figure out how to get everyone through the web. For example, a larger person will need to go through a lower opening by himself, so he can be on the other side to catch the smaller recruits as they are lifted through the higher openings in the web. Let them figure out how to do this as a team without giving any advice.

Obstacle Course Number 3:

Locate a tree with a large overhanging branch from which you can tie and hang a long rope. The rope should hang down to within a few inches of the ground, but not touch the ground. You may need to go to a local park if you don't have a tree like this in your yard. About six feet away from the hanging rope put down a board or short piece of rope to act as a marker. On the opposite side of the hanging rope put another board or rope on the ground, parallel to the first. These two markers represent the edge of a ravine.

Explain to the group that working together they must figure a way to latch onto the hanging rope. They must then use this rope to swing across to the other side without falling into the "bottomless pit" which lies in between. All members must make it across safely. If someone falls in, all must start over. You may want to add an extra challenge by also requiring them to transport an object--such as a bucket of water--to the other side.

This activity is really fun and helps the recruits realize they cannot go through any of these obstacles without helping each other. They must discuss their plans together and then physically aid one another. It is a team effort--everyone needs to make it through the obstacles to win.

# Endurance Contests

Push-ups

Purchase or borrow several tin pie pans and fill them with pudding topped with whipped cream. Just before the contest begins, place one cherry on the top! Choose several recruits to come up and demonstrate their ability to do push-ups. With each push-up they must dip their head into the pie and lap it up, the first one done is the push-up champion!

Bazooka Challenge

Buy several packages of Bazooka bubble gum and give each recruit 3 pieces. They must chew up all three and race to see who can blow the first bubble!

The Sergeant Says

Give everyone a large marshmallow. Then, one at a time, have each person place the marshmallow in his or her mouth and say, "The sergeant says!" Give everyone a second marshmallow and repeat the process. Inform the players that the marshmallows must remain in their mouths and not be swallowed.

Have everyone continue to place more and more marshmallows in their mouths and yell, "The sergeant says." Recruits are eliminated from the competition when they can longer fit any more marshmallows in their mouths or are unable to repeat the phrase. The team that has been able to collectively place the most marshmallows in their mouths wins!

Wheaties Eating Contest

Tell the recruits you need "a few good men" to volunteer. Bring out a bag of Wheaties (or cheap corn flakes), some large serving bowls, extra large spoons, a gallon of milk, and a bowl of sugar. Have the "Men" or "Women" come to the front and sit at the table facing everyone else. Give each volunteer a bowl of cereal and allow him or her to pour the amount of milk they like in their bowl. At the sound of "go" they must eat their cereal as fast as they can. The first one finished with his Wheaties is the strongest and toughest guy or gal around!

 **Skill Contests**

Blind Man's Mission

Lay two 12' ropes on the floor about eight feet apart. Form two teams and have all players remove their shoes. Blindfold two players (one from each team) and spin them around to make them dizzy. Guide them over to their team's rope, so that they are standing barefoot on one end of it. At the signal "GO" each player must feel his way along the rope with his feet. His feet must remain on the rope at all times or he must go back to the beginning and start over again. When he reaches the end of the rope he must take off his blindfold, run back to the start and blindfold the next player on his team. Repeat this until each team member has had a turn. The first team finished wins!

Tug-of-War

Give each person a string that is about six feet long and has a marshmallow tied about six inches from one end. The end of the string nearest to the marshmallow is tied to a chair and the other end is placed in a person's mouth. At the command of "GO" each person begins gathering the string in his mouth (no hands can be used to help) until they reach the marshmallow and begin chewing it up. The first team to have all marshmallows securely embraced in their jaw wins!

Shells or Ammunition

Have each team form a line, one person behind the other. In front of each team, set a row of about twelve unshelled peanuts each about a foot apart. On "Go" the first member of each team gets on his or her knees, they crack open the first peanut and eat it. Then they move to the second peanut, crack it and eat it--and continue in this manner until they have broken open and eaten all twelve peanuts.

While this is taking place one of the judges is placing another line of peanuts on the floor nearby for the next player to crack and eat. When the first team member has the last peanut in his mouth the second team member begins. This continues until all team members have had a turn.

War Games

There are many ways to play war games. You can use old rolled up socks as ammunition and set up boxes in the yard for protection. Or, instead of taking a chance of hurting someone in your group, you can have a marshmallow fight. To do this, divide into two teams and then divide your backyard in half. Lay a rope across the ground to make a dividing line. Give each team a bag of marshmallows to use as ammunition and let the war begin. You cannot cross the line and, similar to dodge ball, once you're hit you are out of the game until the next round begins.

Paper Air Show

Give each recruit a blank sheet of paper and have him or her fold and prepare their own paper airplane. Of course, don't forget to set out the colored markers to decorate and design the planes! Once everyone has finished, have an air show. Each person takes their turn flying and showing off their planes!

War Videos

Some possible movies to watch at the end of the party are **Sergeant Bilko**, **Kelly's Heroes**, and **The Wackiest Ship in the Army** with Don Knotts. Another funny comedy is **Ernest in the Army**.

Icky, Sticky Party

Grotesque Fest

Tell your friends that you are planning a very special evening! They should wear their grubbiest clothes, and they might even want to bring a change of clothes. Give them a specific hour and tell them you would like them to be on time. As they arrive, have them sit down at the table.

Prepare for this meal in advance by covering your table with a plastic tablecloth or disposable paper. On top of this place only glasses or mugs--no silverware, plates, or napkins. Completely cover the table, including the glasses, with a sheet or blanket. After the guests have been seated, remove the sheet or blanket and begin to bring out the food. For the most fun, try using this menu: spaghetti and meat sauce, green salad with dressing, French bread, spinach or corn.

Have your mom and dad serve each person by walking around the table behind them and stopping to plop down a heap of spaghetti directly on the table where the plate should be. Follow this up by placing spaghetti sauce on top. Continue by serving each item on the menu, dropping it directly on the table. They must eat their meal barbarian style, using only their fingers--no forks or spoons allowed! Now the fun begins! Don't forget the camera for some great pictures!

 ## Gooey Balloons

Have everyone choose a partner. Each couple is given a large balloon along with a plastic knife. Instruct them to blow up their balloon and then cover it with shaving cream or whipped cream. One of the team members must hold the balloon while the other team member shaves the balloon. The team with the cleanest balloon wins!

 ## Yuck Toss

Purchase several dozen eggs, and have an egg toss contest. Pair off into couples and hand an egg to one of the partners. Team members face each other and toss the egg back and forth, after each catch taking one step back to add distance to their throws. When their egg "splats" the two are out and must watch the others play!

Oooey Flip Dip

Have each member of your party pair off again. Before the party begins, prepare some chocolate pudding and place it in cups. Hand everyone a cup of pudding and a plastic spoon. The team members sit facing each other, about three feet apart. The first member of the team is to empty his or her cup full of pudding by flipping it with their spoon into their partner's mouth. They "should" be trying to get as much pudding into the "mouth" as they possibly can. Then it is the other person's turn and they must empty their cup!

Blob Painting and Design

Again, pudding is needed for this activity. Make your own pudding paint by using large packages of pudding and powdered milk (cheaper) instead of the real stuff! It is more fun if you have several colors to create with such as: banana, pistachio, Danish Delight, and the old standby chocolate! Then get some large newspaper ends or butcher paper (at the grocery store), and cut off a piece for each person. Have everyone take their shoes off and, using their toes and feet, paint a wonderful picture. The most creative or most highly detailed picture wins!

Head to Head Mess

Have everyone come inside the house and make his or her own delicious sundae. Let them know you are going to eat it outside on the lawn. Have each couple lay head to head and lay their sundae on their chest! Then taking their spoon, they must feed their date the sundae (that was supposed to be theirs) and the other person must feed his sundae to his date!

 ## Slip, Slop, and Slide

Put shaving cream on a plastic slip 'n' slide--and sliiiiiiide! If you don't have a slip and slide, then simply lay down some black plastic—it works just fine. Don't forget to get several cans of shaving cream. This activity is cheap…and fun!

 ## Slop Drop

Purchase one bottle of soda pop for each couple. Then, because canned pop is less expensive, purchase a can of pop for each couple also. Invite one member of each couple to go ahead and drink the bottled pop. Then, have him lie on the ground with his partner standing above him, near his head. The person lying on the ground places a towel over his chest and shoulders and must hold the empty pop bottle up to his mouth. You can use your hands to hold the pop bottle. Holding the can of pop about waist high, his partner then pours the can of pop into the empty bottle. The couple that fills the pop bottle the fullest wins!

 ## Mush Face Wash

Purchase a box of instant oatmeal, the kind with the individual serving packets. Let each couple choose two packets. Have them pour the packets into a bowl, add water, and cook in a microwave using the directions on the back of the package. Set all the bowls of oatmeal in the refrigerator for awhile to cool off. After the oatmeal has become nice and cold and gooey, have the girls give the guys nice "masks" by plastering the oatmeal on their partner's face and letting it dry a few minutes. Then equip each girl with a squirt gun and have her stand in front of her partner. Using only the squirt gun, the couple that can get the entire Mush Mask off first is the winner!

 ## Sticky Human Sundae

Split the group into two teams and ask for a volunteer from each. (Don't tell anyone in advance what you are about to have him or her do, or you will not get any volunteers!) Bring out two lawn chairs and set them on the grass—one in front of each group. Explain that this is a very serious and very artistic competition--one that all present will long remember! Then ask the two volunteers to be seated. Next, give each person on both teams one item that can be used to create an ice cream sundae such as: a can of chocolate syrup, a bottle of caramel or strawberry topping, a can of whipped cream or chopped nuts, or a bottle of maraschino cherries. Everyone must empty his or her sundae condiments on the head of the "human sundae" volunteer. The best looking sundae wins!

 ## Clean up!

The funniest part of the whole party is hosing everyone off!

Hunk Hunt

This party is for a group of teenage girls—or, if you have a group of teenage boys, call it a chick hunt. This scavenger hunt is especially fun because at the end of the hunt, you have gathered together some big hunks that are just sitting at home bored, and you have also included other kids in your party that you might not have normally invited!

Divide into two teams and give each team a list, such as the following:

Find a "hunk of a guy" who:

1. Speaks Spanish
2. Wears size 11 shoes

3. Who plays football on the school team
4. Drives a hot motorcycle
5. Plays a musical instrument
6. Goes home at lunch
7. Is a class officer
8. Has gotten a track award of some type
9. Attended the same grade school as at least 2 of you
10. Has red hair
11. Works after school
12. Has big blue eyes
13. Is in your Sunday school class

Convince the "hunks" or guys to come over and join in some fun—or, if you can't...then at least have them sign their name on the paper behind the requirement. Once you have your group back together, and if you have some "hunks" with you, watch a good "guy" video. Proclaim the winners (the group that brought back the most guys) and give each person on the team a "Big Hunk" (candy bar) to take home with them!

Out to Dinner

It's always fun to "eat out" and this will be the most unique meal and unique place you will ever eat! Prepare the group by getting them excited about going "out to dinner". After everyone is in the car, drive around for awhile, discussing places where you might like to eat. Then tell them you have a great idea. You know a place where they have never eaten before!

While you are driving around, by previous arrangement have your family set up a table on a traffic island somewhere in town or next to the highway in a highly visible park. The table should be covered with a nice table cloth and candles. Place some batteries in your CD player and have some nice, soft dinner music playing in the background. Then light the candles and explain that your meal will soon be delivered.

As previously arranged have several friends or parents "deliver" the meal to you in their car. Give them the food that you want delivered and instruct them to drive by and throw one dinner item out the window to you about every five to seven minutes.

As they drive by the first time, have them throw out a large, plastic Ziploc bag that contains plates, cups, plastic silverware and a note that says: "Here's your thrown together dinner!" On the next pass they will throw out the car window a "tossed" salad with a plastic jar of dressing.

As they speed by on subsequent runs they will deliver "Smashed Sandwiches" "Squished Chips"--"Pitched Punch"--with "Hurled Jell-O" for dessert. At the end of the meal, they will pass by and throw a game out of the window for you to play!

Daffy Dinner

Before dinner, prepare a small slip of paper for each person to read and place it under their plates. On these slips of paper are written specific instructions for each of them. After everyone is seated at the table, instruct them to read the slip of paper under their plate. Explain that during the meal, each person must carry out the instructions they have been given. For example, one note might say: "Whenever Megan laughs, glare at her and eat something off the plate of someone next to you."

Instructions to others might be: "When Chary picks up a knife, answer the telephone." "When Tyler takes a drink, run around the table acting like a gorilla." "Everytime someone takes a second helping, snort like a pig." "When someone puts their elbows on the table, yell 'Oh, no!'" "Whenever Logan eats a piece of chicken, stand up and curtsey." "When someone says another person's name, flip water on them from your glass." "When anyone says something mean, spank them."

During the meal each person closely watches the actions of the others, and everyone will have a great time trying to figure out what he or she thinks the instructions were on each slip of paper.

Boob-Tube Marathon

Once in awhile, it's fun to sit in front of the boob tube, have tons of snacks, and pull an all-niter! Of course, this has to be an "all boys" party, or an "all girls" party if it goes all night! What will make this movie marathon even more fun is to have a theme. For example, you may want to watch all the **Rocky** movies in one night, or the four **Star Wars** movies, or have an **Indiana Jones** marathon. If there are ladies involved, **Pride and Prejudice** is wonderful, or the **Anne of Green Gable** and **Anne of Avonlee** series. When you are choosing...don't forget to consider Alfred Hitchcock's great suspense movies! Pull out the sleeping bags and pillows and food and go to it!

An Indian Pow Wow

If you live in the West, you have had many opportunities to play "Cowboys and Indians" over the years! But since you have matured...you probably have given up such fun! But an Indian Party is a great theme party; one I'll bet no one else has done, or ever will!

American Indian attire is pretty easy to find, or just have each person make their own costume using paper sacks. You can construct vests, and the guys can make a loin clothe to wear over their jeans! If available in your area, I recommend Deseret Industries or another thrift store to find something very "Indianish" to wear. You can purchase feathered head-dresses at WalMart or at a party shop. Finding a teepee to put up in your backyard would add to the fun! Ask around-- you might be surprised to discover that someone you know might have one.

War Paint

Ask your mom if she has any leftover Halloween make-up. Stick make-up works the best, but if not use old lipstick and dark eye shadow (ask first please). Or, buy some cheap makeup--it will also work okay. Once all the kids have arrived, begin to transform yourselves into mean looking braves and squaws! It's fun to have the guys paint the girls and the girls paint the guys!

Pre-Ordeal

Before you begin the actual hunting-for-white-man "ordeal", perhaps you could use some practice in archery! Purchase for about $3.99 bow and arrow kits at WalMart or at a local toy store, (toy ones with the rubber tips on the end of the arrows). Set up bales of hay, or even attach some pictures to the backyard fence for a target. It might be fun to chew on jerky while you are refining your excellent bow and arrow marksmanship!

Hunt for the White Man

Is your younger brothers and sisters, or the little kids across the street been driving you crazy for some time now? Well, this is a great activity for revenge.... **You need white man to hunt!**

In the early planning stages of this date, line up several white men (children) for you and your friends to hunt down and scalp! Split into teams of two, and give each brave and squaw a plastic bow and arrow (with rubber tips) and decide which white man is theirs to hunt! Then go to a pretty wilderness area, a park, or a nearby campground where the white man can hide and run freely! Each team has to count to 100 before the hunt begins. Then the white man must be hunted down, shot, and carried back to the car! After the hunt is over, don't forget to thank the little white fellows for being so brave!

 ## Ceremonial Dinner

Have a younger brother or sister dress up in a ceremonial Indian costume (head-dress, war paint, and a loin cloth) to serve you dinner in the backyard. If you could not find a teepee, eat your meal sitting Indian style on the ground. Purchase some picnic plates (woven plates to put under paper plates) at WalMart and eat with your hands!

 ## Easy Navajo Tacos

2 cups flour
1 cup milk
1 Tbs. baking powder

Mix together to make a dough. Pull off enough to make a 2-inch ball. Roll flat and cook in about ½ inch hot oil in a skillet. Lay the fried scone flat on a plate and cover with chili, hamburger, cheese, lettuce, onions and sour cream.

Also serve "laughing water" (punch) for a drink.

 ## Legends

Sit around a fire and have someone read old Indian legends. Other activities could be canoeing down the river with your squaws, doing American Indian dances around a fire, or if you know someone with horses, go bareback riding!

 ## Native American video

There are so many wonderful videos to rent about the lives and history of Native Americans. **I will Fight No More Forever, Windwalker, Crazy Horse,** and **Against a Crooked Sky** are just a few you could choose.

Submarine Races

This is a great date if you live near or around a lake or river. It will take some preparation however, because several weeks prior to this activity you will need to ask the manager of an appliance store to save freezer or refrigerator boxes for you. Sailor hats are cheap and can be found at party shops if you want to add some character to the races. You will need one large cardboard box per couple. Have on hand plenty of poster paints, paint brushes, and duct tape, and knives or scissors to cut cardboard. Instruct each couple that they are to design and make their own submarine. Let them know that prizes will be awarded for "best design," "best decorated," and, of course, the grand prize of "the longest floating submarine."

Once the submarines have been designed and decorated, they are ready to be tested in the water. Grab some rope, load the boats into the back of a pickup, and head for the water for the submarine races! Once at the lake or river, one person must be aboard the sub (don't forget the lifejackets) and the other person uses the rope on shore to keep the boat from floating away and to keep his fellow sailor alive! The last "Sub" to stay afloat is the winner!

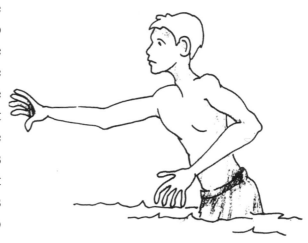

Following the races, it might then be fun to go to a local park. Have the fixings ready for everyone to make their own submarine sandwich. Add some chips, salad, and pop!

Dinner in a Yacht

During the summer months it is always fun to eat out in a yacht! Yacht, you say? Who has a yacht that I know? Well, I didn't actually mean a "yacht," I meant a boat, but I said a "yacht" because it is more exciting than telling you to eat in a boat! If your family does not have a motor boat, I am sure you know several people who have one and wouldn't mind you having some fun with it! Ask if you can use their boat for the evening and let them know that you won't even be taking it out of their driveway! Now use your imaginations and figure out a real fun meal to eat in a boat. I would suggest something "fishy" like Fish and Chips and cold slaw. Add a few little gummy fish to float in your drink!

Also, it might be fun to have your younger brother or sister take your orders and serve you wearing a sailor hat and a lifejacket or swimsuit and goggles! Following dinner, watch a movie in your yacht. Set up a small TV and your family VCR in the boat. Movie possibilities include **The Wackiest Ship in the Army, South Pacific,** or **On the Beach**!

Water Works

Have you ever thought of just having a "pool party" during the summer at your local swimming pool, either inside or outside? Or, it's fun to go to a nearby lake. Everyone loves to go swimming here are some great ideas to keep the party moving and fun!

Water Spots

Everyone has a pair of sunglasses, but the problem with wearing them in the water is…you can't really see out of them very well when someone splashes water on you! Here's a contest you can have throughout the whole Water Works party! Once your guests have entered the water, each person may not remove their sunglasses again! They can wipe off the glasses with their hands or wet suit or T-shirt, but they can never remove them from their head! At the end of the party, award the sunglass winners (those who do not remove their glasses the whole time) with a wet wipe to wash off the water spots!

In and Out

Everyone must bring their own water tube or small boat to the water party! Have each person stand on their floaty and at the sound of go, jump off and get back on. Do this several times, and see who can do it the fastest each time!

Shirt On and Off

Bring two old, large T-shirts to play this relay game. Line everyone up in the water in two lines. Team members should be about four feet from each other. Start at the beginning of the line and hand the first person a wet T-shirt to put on. Then, he or she takes it off and throws it to the next person in his line. They, in turn, put on the T-shirt and take it off again. Continue in this manner until everyone has had on the wet T-shirt. The winner is the team that finishes first!

 ## Nose Cool Off

Have several balloons blown up and ready to use. Give each person his own balloon and show them where the start and finish lines are for this race. If you are using a swimming pool for your race course then use the rope in the pool as the finish line. Each person must push their balloon using their nose. The winner is the first one who crosses the line with his or her balloon!

 ## Bobbing for Rubber Duckies

Purchase two small hula hoops at WalMart or another similar store in your area. Also look for cheap rubber duckies that will float in the water, or use several lightweight Nerf balls. Have two people lay on the side of the pool. Place the hula hoops in the pool and the rubber duckies or Nerf balls inside the hula hoops. The two contestants must lean over the edge of the pool and using their teeth only bob for the duckies and spit them out on the deck! The hula hoops keep the duckies in place during the contest! First one to get all the duckies out of the pool wins!

Wet Shirt Keep Away!

It is always fun to play keep away! Using one of the T-shirts you have already used, divide into two teams and play keep away throwing the wet shirt back and forth.

Nerf Baseball

Play a rousing game of baseball in the pool! Use some of your guests or younger brothers or sisters as the bases. Divide up into two teams and, using a Nerf ball and a small tennis racket as the bat, play a game of baseball!

Come Have a Ball

As soon as spring has sprung, take advantage of the nice weather and have a sports marathon! Start out by playing baseball at the local park. It is fun to play with a plastic ball and bat. Then play some volleyball--or stretch a string across the living room of your house and play balloon volleyball.

Next, you may want to play flag football. For the flags, simply cut some 15" strips of fabric. Tuck them two inches inside the pants at the waist, allowing the flags to hang down over the hips. Also, if available, go to the local pool and swim...or play soccer at the park. You may even wish to add a quick game of basketball to this gala event.

That evening, following a vigorous day of physical fun, have an all-American meal! Hot dogs, root beer in a can, a bag of potato chips, and an ice cream cone!

Everyone's Evening

Sometimes school dances can be so boring! Here is an idea that I bet none of your friends has ever tried! Get a group of your friends together and go on a great group date to the dance! Decide whom you want to ask to the school dance. Now remember that you have to like everyone who is going on this date, because everyone of the opposite sex is your date at some point during the evening!

First of all, each of you should ask the girl or guy of your choice creatively! There are many books on the subject of asking someone to a dance. Check out some of these books and come up with a great creative way to ask your date!

You have decided you want to ask Jane to the dance and you do it. Now when it is time for you to order flowers, you ask Susan, who was asked by someone else going in your group what color of dress she is wearing to the dance. You then buy the corsage for Susan and pin it on her or give her the wrist corsage at the beginning of the date.

In the car sit by a different girl than the one you asked and got the flowers for. Then during the dinner, you pull the chair out and sit by Stacy and act as her date during the meal.

During the dance you dance with each girl in your group, and then on the way home you sit by Kerri and walk her up to the doorstep and thank her for the great evening! Be sure to take some great "group pictures" instead of single couple pictures…since you actually went to the dance with EVERYONE!

Nostalgia

Relive childhood with your friends by spending the afternoon in the park climbing trees, playing on the playground equipment, eating peanut butter sandwiches and drinking chocolate milk.

If your park has a small stream or pond, construct boats using a bar of Ivory soap, tying tree twigs together, or by using lightweight blocks of wood. Build dams and wade in the water together. Then spend some time sitting on a blanket telling some of your favorite childhood memories!

Drive-In Fun

One of the most fun activities you can do during the summer months is to go to the drive-in! Wait for a great movie and load up the lawn chairs, blankets, popcorn, and soda pop! If you live in a farming community, it is great fun to get a large grain truck that can be tipped up! Load the truck with some straw or cottonseed and some blankets, and back into the last row of the drive-in. Tip up the bed of the truck and then cram in as many kids as you can. Use your battery-powered radio and tune into the channel and enjoy!

Or…if you own a pickup truck, park it backwards and set up the lawn chairs in the back for everyone to sit on. If you don't own a truck, simply set up the chairs in front of the car, wrap up in blankets, enjoy your treats, and turn up the speakers! Together, sit back and enjoy the movie, the fresh air, and the mosquitoes!

A Mud Fest

A Mud Fest is a great summer activity! Find or make a slick muddy area. You can use your garden spot just before planting. Or, wait until mid-summer when the river or reservoir water gets low and the mud on the banks is nice and thick. Perhaps your area has a "mud bog" car-racing contest at the county fair. Wait until the big event is over, and then the next day go down and use the already prepared area!

Have everyone dress in their grubbies (cut-off blue jeans work well) and have a mud fight, play tug-of-war, and mud football (tackle football)! Other activities could include a mud flinging contest, a best mud pie contest, or a mud hair-do contest! Be sure that everyone is covered in mud from head to toe!

Following the frolic, load the kids in the back of a pickup and go home and wash down every one with the garden hose. Then serve Mud Pies!

Recipe for Mud Pies

1/3 cup cocoa
4 eggs
1-1/2 cups flour
2 tsp. Vanilla
1-pkg. mini marshmallows
2 cubes margarine
2 cups sugar

Frosting: 1/2 cube margarine, 1-1/2 cups powdered sugar, 1/3 cup cocoa, 1/3 cup milk.

Combine the margarine, sugar, and cocoa. Add the eggs and remaining ingredients except the marshmallows. Cook in a long rectangular pan or on a cookie sheet for thirty minutes at 375 degrees. Remove from the oven and cool. Spread the package of marshmallows on and return to the oven for about three minutes, allowing the marshmallows to swell. Remove from the oven and cool for one-half hour. Then frost and refrigerate.

Mission Impossible

Here's a really fun, creative group activity to do during the afternoon before a special dance. It takes some preparation, but it's worth it. Either a group of girls or a group of boys can arrange this for their dates. For our example here, we will have the boys arranging and planning the date....

TOP SECRET Video

During the week before the dance, the boys begin by making a "mission impossible" home video. A father of one boy should act as the narrator while mission impossible music (from the video of the movie) plays in the background. Have the dad wear a hat and videotape him from behind so his face is not shown, while he is sitting in a large chair. He uses a deep voice and tells the girls that their dates have been kidnapped. Foreign agents from Russia have abducted them. These agents are dangerous and are holding the boys hostage for possible ransom. He then holds up a picture of each boy, one at a time, and states their name and "alias." After each picture is shown, the video fades out and shifts to a scene that shows that particular boy being captured by masked thugs. Play suspenseful music in the background and use your creativity here to think of different situations where and how each boy is abducted. Possible abductions could be: taken from a basketball game while playing in the gym, taken from the shower in their own home, abducted while at work and taken hostage. Use your imagination, and your acting abilities!

After showing a picture of each boy, and then showing how their kidnapping took place, the narrator then tells the "ladies" that the agents will be contacting the girls shortly with instructions for them to follow if they ever want to see their dates again. The girls' "mission" is to find and free their dates from the evil foreign agents so that they can go with them to the dance tonight. The tape finishes by giving the girls instructions specific to your area, such as, "You will be receiving a phone call at exactly 3:30 p.m. at the telephone outside the Mini Mart convenience store on 1st Street with the first clue as to the boys' whereabouts. Good luck with your mission, ladies. This tape will self-destruct in exactly ten seconds."

TOP SECRET Following the Clues

During the week prior to the dance, the girls are told to meet at one of the girl's homes by 3:00 p.m. and told that the boys will meet them there for a fun afternoon of activities. While waiting for the arrival of the boys, the doorbell rings and the girls find a videotape on the porch with a note attached instructing them to play it. This, of course, is the mission impossible video previously described.

1ˢᵗ Stop, Gas and Go Stop, 3:30pm

The instructions the boys give will be specific for your particular community, of course. For the purpose of our example here, the girls follow the instructions from the videotape and drive to the Mini Mart by 3:30 p.m. so they can be there to receive the phone call. (One of the mothers could accompany the girls with a video camera, recording the girls' adventure, so the entire group can enjoy it later, after the dance.) The boys will have previously obtained the phone number of this pay telephone and at 3:30 p.m. one of the boys will make the phone call. Using a deep, raspy voice with a foreign accent, he will give the girls instructions. He should have previously written out exactly what he will say. Here is an example:

"We have the boys and if you want them you must do exactly what we tell you to do! Before we give you further instructions and to make sure you have not involved the police, you have exactly 5 minutes to be at the pay phone at the Texaco station by the high school, where we will tell you how to proceed and where to go!"

2ⁿᵈ Stop, a Gas Station, 3:40 p.m.

The boys should have the script for each phone call previously written out, and the exact time and phone number for the telephone call to be made. Giving the girls sufficient time to get to the next destination (ten minutes), the next boy calls the telephone outside the Texaco station and might say: "We have the boys hostage and have decided to demand a ransom if you want them by the time the dance starts. You must do exactly as I say, and if there is any funny business, any police involved, we will take the boys immediately out of the country and as far away from you as possible! We are demanding a ransom of exactly $5.00 in American money. It must be dropped off at a destination that will be given to you later. We want you to deliver the money in a red attaché case that can be found hidden under the overpass on Cedar Drive. Once you have found this briefcase we want the money placed in it in small, unmarked coins. We want exactly 65 pennies, 32 nickels, 15 dimes, and 5 quarters. We will give you one-half hour in which to get this money together and will contact you by telephone at exactly 4:15 p.m. at the I.G.A. on Market Street to tell you where we want the money dropped."

3ʳᵈ Stop, Grocery Store 4:15 p.m.

The next boy calls the I.G.A. and, says: "You have the money, I presume? Well, well! Now go directly to the pioneer statue in Grant Park and hide the attaché case in the bushes. We are watching every step you make. We don't want any funny business, and after the drop, if it goes without incident, we will tell you where the boys are hidden. You will find a letter in the bushes where you leave the cash with further instructions."

4ᵗʰ Stop, A Letter in the park

The letter inside the envelope reads: We have changed our minds! You can keep your money! It is not enough. We would rather have your boys! If you want to see these guys again, you'll have to find them. This is no trick…your next clue is in a treat! Put on Halloween costumes and go door-to-door looking for the candy with a clue! Be very careful not to swallow the clue. The following houses are where you are to go trick-or-treating:

453 Evans
830 Easy Circle
780 Yates
1721 Iowa Circle

(Previously arrange for these parents to have candy ready for the girls.)

The clue is inside peanut M&M candy. Crack the M&M's in the microwave and take out the peanut and replace with a small piece of paper that has one letter in each peanut. (You do this by putting one peanut M&M in the microwave at a time for about 30 seconds, then quickly remove the nut while it is warm, put the note inside and close it back up so that the chocolate melts it back together.) It might take several times to get it right, but with practice and a few tries, it works great!

The clues inside the pieces of candy spell the words "Recreation Center." The mom with the girls can tell them that they had better take their swimsuits and towels just in case! They then ask at the swimming pool front desk for the note that has been left for them.

At Community Swimming Pool

Inside the envelope at the Recreation Center front desk are entrance passes for each girl plus a note that says:

"Give the attendant these entrance passes. Put on your swimsuits. You will find a key at the bottom of the swimming pool at the 7-foot marker. Retrieve the key. It will open a locker where you will find a brown paper bag and your next clue!"

(This clue and paper bag will be inside a locker in the boys' locker room. The girls will need to get a boy to open it and bring them the message and the bag.)

The bag will contain party hats and cupcakes. The clue inside the locker will state: "Go to McDonald's, put on these hats and pretend to be having a birthday party. Once you start singing 'Happy Birthday' someone will approach you and give you your next clue."

A clown, or someone even just wearing a silly colored wig (your younger brother or sister), hands the girls the final clue in an envelope that tells them where their men are tied up and awaiting rescue.

Once the girls have reached the last destination with the final clue, they should find the boys tied and gagged and waiting for their rescuers! Then take the girls back to their homes to get ready for the dance and enjoy a wonderful evening, watching the video afterwards!

Jingle Bell Blast

🎄 Santa's a Hostage

Sometime after this holiday party has begun have a parent ring the front doorbell and quickly leave. The person answering the door will find a piece of Santa's outfit (such as a red hat) on the porch along with a ransom note informing your guests that SANTA has been kidnapped and taken hostage! The most fun person to act the part of the kidnapped St. Nick might be your dad or mom dressed up in a Santa suit (borrowed from the church or a friend). But if this is not possible and your parents refuse to spend the evening tied up out in the cold, you could even hide a stuffed Santa to search and find!

Send your group on a wild goose chase, all over town, giving them clues to Santa's whereabouts! Use some fun ideas similar to those described in the "Mission Impossible" date—such as, phone calls to pay telephones, dropping off money in a brief case, and perhaps some other clues that take some thought to figure out.

At the end of the search, have Santa tied up and gagged with some fun Christmas treat in his bag for the good little boys and girls who came to his rescue and saved the day! This can be a fun mystery search for Santa and one that your friends will never forget if you put some thought and work into it!

Snowman Decorating Contest

This is a contest of skill and creativity! The boys will act as the snowmen and the girls will do the decorating! Give each girl a can of whipped cream, a man (her date), a bowl of candies, frosting tips with frosting of various colors, a butter knife, and a hat of some sort! Each "man" must sit on a chair while the girl applies the whipped cream to the back of his head! Now for the creative stuff she must make "her man's head" the best looking snowman of the bunch! Have your mom, dad, or a sibling judge the contest! Don't forget to take pictures because the poor snowmen really can't see what is going on behind their backs...I mean heads!

Carol Lip Sync

There are some great Christmas songs out today, some that have a really fun beat and others that are real crackup! Santa Got Runover By A Reindeer, Jingle Bell Rock, and even the great song Jingle Bells being barked out by dogs! Make a mental note to listen to and find some great music for this party! You can ask the radio station to play the music and then record it. A lip sync is more successful when you let the groups know well in advance what they will be performing so they can gather their props, come up with costumes and instruments, and practice a bit before they go on stage!

Rhyming Game

This is a great game and one your mom will want you to play. Why? Because this game requires a clean and tidy house! In this game, if you have a lot of things just lying around and not put away, your friends will become confused. Your mom will greatly appreciate your help with the cleaning!

Give each person a pencil and piece of paper, or divide into groups of two or three people working together. Place articles around the house in pairs. These articles must rhyme (see examples listed below). Most of these items can be purchased in the "trinket" or novelty Christmas section of your local department store. Each individual or group must find the articles, figure out what they are and how they rhyme, and then write it down. This game should have a time limit of perhaps 30 minutes. When the time is up, gather everyone together and read your list of correct answers. See who has found and correctly rhymed the most.

Examples:

1. Ball in hall (suspend round Christmas ornament from hallway ceiling)
2. Bill on sill (place a dollar bill on a window sill)
3. Cone on phone (pinecone on telephone)
4. Cutter on butter (cookie cutter on a stick of butter or margarine)

5. Flock on clock.
6. Bow in snow (Christmas bow laying on batting or cotton)
7. Dime on chime (a dime taped onto doorbell chime)
8. Elf on shelf
9. Deer on mirror (tape miniature toy deer on mirror)
10. Sled on bed
11. Frog on log (miniature toy frog on fireplace log)
12. Pickle on sickle (use ice sickles used on Christmas trees)
13. Lights on tights (Christmas lights on child's tights)
14. Limb on brim (small tree limb on brim of a hat)
15. Holly on dolly (Christmas holly on a doll)
16. Bear on chair (use teddy bear, not live bear!)
17. Bell on shell (Christmas bell on sea shell or shell of egg)
18. Star on jar (Christmas star on cookie jar)
19. Cap on tap (bottle cap on kitchen sink tap)
20. Spoon on tune (place a spoon on top of your piano)
21. Note on coat (note to Santa on top of a coat)
22. Rock on sock (rock on Christmas stocking)
23. Key on tree (hang a key on Christmas tree)
24. Spice on rice (container of cinnamon on a box of rice)
25. Gift on sift (wrapped package on top of floursifter
26. Man on can (snowman on a can of something)
27. Ring on string (canning ring hung by string from a doorknob)
28. Nick on pick (St. Nick sitting on a toothpick)
29. Handle on candle (screwdriver handle on candle)
30. Fruit on boot (apple on snow boot)
31. Vase on case (flower vase on bookcase)
32. Teeth on wreath
33. Doves on gloves

Halloween Hysteria

Halloween is a great time to plan a creative date or party! It is especially fun to do on Halloween night, since most...I said most...of you have outgrown Trick-or-Treating and this party will give you and your friends something to do! Don't forget to enlist other parents to help you with the fun Halloween meal.

Blindfold your guests and lead them to the middle of a field, a backyard with several trees or to a graveyard (get permission first). Ask your parents or family members to have everything set up and ready when you arrive. Have scary music playing on a portable tape player and have a lantern or candle lit on the table. Have a ghost (a parent) welcome them as they arrive and have a monster (a parent) seat them and serve them dinner.

Fun Halloween Dinner Ideas

**Dinner in a Pumpkin

Dinner is a great time to start a holiday celebration. Begin preparations for your special Halloween dinner by cleaning out the inside of a fairly large-sized pumpkin and then use a black magic marker to draw a silly, smiling face on it.

Use this as a "serving dish," placing the previously prepared main course of your Halloween dinner inside. (Note: Do not "cook" your dinner inside the pumpkin because it will take on the pumpkin's taste!) Some possible entrees include spaghetti, beef stroganoff, or stew.

**Pumpkin Burgers:

Cut out jack-o-lanterns from slices of cheese using a cookie cutter. Cook your normal hamburgers, place on a bun and place the cheese on top.

**Pumpkin Pizza:

A quick and easy to make "pumpkin dinner" can be had by simply purchasing a round cheese pizza at your local grocery store. Make a face on the pizza using black olives which have been cut in half. Make the stem at the top using a green pepper. Pop in oven and then serve!

**Halloween Punch:

Purchase a pair of plastic gloves at your local hardware store. Fill one glove with water and place in freezer overnight. When ready for use, cut off plastic and place hand-shaped ice cube in punch bowl. Or, it's fun to have spiders in your punch. Do this by purchasing plastic spider rings, washing them, and placing them in ice cube trays. Pour water over the top and place in freezer. Drop ices cubes in the glass and fill with punch.

**Goblin Salad:

Use cookie cutters shaped like pumpkins, witches, and ghosts to cut slices of cheese into Halloween figures. Place these figures on top of individual serving plates of green salad...or on top of a bowl of chili.

** Tombstone Ice Creme

Try this for dessert. Purchase a half-gallon of vanilla ice cream. Completely unwrap the ice cream from its carton. Slice the ice cream into rectangular blocks, each block large enough to serve one person. Place the blocks of ice cream on a serving tray, one block for each person. Crush a bag of Oreo cookies using a rolling pin. This will become your **"dirt."** Place this **"dirt"** over each block of ice cream, pressing gently into the ice cream by using your hands. Now you have made a "grave" for each person. Using white poster board cut out small tombstones. On the tombstone, use black marker to write "R.I.P." which means, "Rest in Peace" and under this write each persons name. By gently pressing, attach one of these tombstones onto the end of each of the graves. Place the serving tray in the freezer until it's time for dessert, and then present each person with his or her own personalized "grave."

**Table decorations

Decorate your table by covering with an orange tablecloth (or you can buy orange-colored butcher paper at your local office supply and tape it to your table). Spread Halloween-colored candy corn all over the table.

Trick -or -Treat game

Have everyone sit on the living room floor in a circle. Each person takes a turn reaching into a Halloween bag (or plastic pumpkin if you have one) and drawing out a piece of paper on which has been written a note.

On some notes are written, "You get a TREAT." If this is drawn, they are given a miniature candy bar, or other treat that has been prepared. On other slips of paper are written the descriptions of "TRICKS" which the person drawing it must perform.

Place equal numbers of "TRICKS" or "TREATS" in the bag. You may wish to increase the action by having people race each other in certain events. This gives more of you a chance to participate in the fun. Following are a sample of some "TRICKS"!

1 - Eat a hanging donut (hang donut from ceiling so person will have to stand on toes to reach it with their mouth--they must eat without using hands)

2 - Squirt out a candle (light candle in jack-o-lantern, move person back 3 steps from candle, blindfold, spin them around; they must extinguish candle using squirt gun)

3 - Move the cotton balls (put cotton balls in bowl, blindfold & use spoon to get them all into another bowl)

4 - Recite a favorite poem...dramatically (Mary had a Little Lamb, or Twinkle, Twinkle Little Star)

5 - Blind elephants (blindfold two people--one shells and feeds peanuts to partner)

6 - Eat a pie without using hands (put chocolate pie filling topped with whipped cream in pie plate

7 - Do a witch dance (put on a witch hat, hold a broom, and dance to Halloween music)

8 - Shave someone's legs (use butter knife & shaving cream, wipe knife on towel)

9 - Put 5 pieces of bubble gum in your mouth, chew & blow a large bubble

10 - Put on 20 shirts, one over the top of the other

11 - Walk across room with pillow between knees, coin in one eye & plate on head

12 - Drink a baby bottled filled with Kool-Aid

13 - Everyone gets to squirt you with a squirt gun 4 times

14 - Walk across the room barefoot with marbles between your toes

15 - Have others wrap you up like a mummy using toilet paper

16 - Eat a "Big Hunk" candy bar within 5 minutes

17 - Choose someone to "fix" your hair (use spray can of washable hair dye, curling iron, etc.)

18 - See if you can put twelve marshmallows in your mouth at one time

19 - Suck pumpkin seeds with a straw and move the seeds from one bowl to another (race with another person)

20 - Must take a walk outside in the dark...alone

21 - "Bob" for baby pumpkins in a witch kettle (use small pumpkin gourds)

22 - Choose a partner for yourself and then choose two other individuals who will act as partners to compete against. See who can empty a can of whipped cream into their partner's mouth the fastest

Little Tea Party

    Words like little, small, and miniature, are the words and activities you will be using for the evening! For this little tea party, you might have to borrow a few items from families you know who have small children living at home. Borrow a small table and chair set, and some dolly dishes! Oh, you also need to borrow the actual little children themselves to serve your little meal, at your little tea party! Of course, little girls work best, plus they will have fun and love doing it!

    Set up the table and chairs on a little hill somewhere. Then place a little tablecloth on the table and use little birthday candles as your candles. A few little dandelions in the center of the table would look nice, too! Add the little dishes and cups and silverware and you are ready for your meal!

Beforehand, have your mom fix a little meal, "little" meaning not much food, because your dishes are small and you can't put a lot of food on them! Have the little children wearing Sunday best, carrying a white linen napkin, serve you the meal. Don't forget to play some of your favorite music like nursery rhyme songs, or "It's a Small World After All" over and over and over--or use Primary songs in the background. Now you are ready for the dessert! How about roasting little miniature marshmallows on toothpicks over the candles on your table?

Following the tea party, play some little games like "Hi Ho Cherry -O" or "Chutes and Ladders." Or, perhaps go miniature golfing, or swim in a little wadding pool!

Chocolate Night

Do you personally know kids that are choco-holics? Well, you might want to invite them to this party! Doesn't everyone have a craving for chocolate every once in awhile? After this fun evening, I'm betting you will be satisfied for a long time! This party involves chocolate...and I mean a lot of chocolate!

Chocolate Drop

Begin the party by dividing into groups of two's. Make one member of the team the chocolate dropper and the other member the receiver. Put newspaper or plastic down on the floor and a garbage bag over the receiver's clothes. The receiver lies on the floor; the dropper stands directly over the head of his partner with 6 large marshmallows and a dish of chocolate syrup. The dropper dips each marshmallow into the syrup and then drops the chocolate marshmallow one at a time into his partners' mouth. The best shot wins!

Progressive Bake

During this part of the activity, you will be traveling from house to house with your friends testing and baking their favorite chocolate treats! Don't forget to have everyone bring an apron, because they will need it! It is important that each person has all the ingredients at home and the recipe ready, so that when you arrive you can put on your aprons and help them bake their favorite treat!

Once you have mixed, baked, and cleaned up your mess then it is time to sample! Jump back into the car and head to the next home to bake and taste again!

Winter Frolic

Have everyone come in warm clothes and get your snow shovels and brooms out for a morning of fun. Before your friends or neighbors are up and about, shovel their walks and driveways. Then it's time for snow fun and games!

You may want to start by building a snowman, making snow sculptures, and playing fox and geese at the park. Make a target and give every one ten tries to hit it with a snowball. Have an icicle hunt for the weirdest shape, the longest, the smallest, the fattest, etc.

Next, play miniature snow golf. Bury plastic or Styrofoam cups in the snow. Use light, plastic golf balls or make your own golf balls out of snow. Then, using a plastic club or putter, play a round or two. Following the festivities, head home for hot chocolate, Hostess Snowballs, and a great feeling!